First among Losers

First among Losers

Robin and Chris Lawrie

Illustrated by
Robin Lawrie

Evans

Acknowledgements

The authors and publishers would like to thank Julia Francis, Hereford Diocesan Deaf Church lay co-chaplain, for her help with the sign language in the *Chain Gang* books, and Dr Cathy Turtle, ecologist, for her help with the selection of species in books 13 to 18.

Published by Evans Brothers Limited
2A Portman Mansions
Chiltern Street
London W1U 6NR

© Robin and Christine Lawrie
First published 2004

The authors assert their moral right to be identified as the authors of this work in accordance with the Copyright, Designs and Patents Act, 1988.

Printed in Hong Kong

British Library Cataloguing in Publication data.
Lawrie, Robin
First among Losers. – (The Chain Gang)
1. Slam Duncan (Fictitious character) – Juvenile fiction
2. All terrain cycling – Juvenile fiction 3. Adventure stories
4. Children's stories
I. Title II. Lawrie, Chris
823.9'14[J]

ISBN 0 237 525623

Hi, my name is 'Slam' Duncan. I ride and race downhill mountain bikes with a group of other kids. This is Aziz, – we call him 'Dozy'. This is Fionn. Then there's Larry and Andy. We call ourselves 'The Chain Gang'.

We practise and race on a hill called Westridge behind the village where we live. Some property developers want to put houses on it. They stopped us using our favourite courses where they want to build, so we made a new course on the other side of the hill.

*I'm Andy. (Andy is deaf. He signs instead of talking.)

5

The new course goes over an old quarry
so we had to build lots of aerial rampways
and flyovers to cross
the rough terrain.

One of the toughest jumps
is called 'the Dragon'.
Someone stuck teeth shapes
and old headlamps for eyes
on it to make it even scarier.

If you don't get it just right . . .

. . . you could have a hard landing.
To avoid problems like this the
Chain Gang were training together
and sharing information.
We wanted to be ready for
the next Westridge
race meeting.

Brake before the drop.

Pre-jump here.

Keep your front wheel up here.

Lean back here.

*Land here.

Our main rival, Punk Tuer, was training with a bunch of no-hopers who never helped each other.

But, of course, Punk doesn't need to do much training. He can win races just by having the very latest bike technology.

His dad owns a shop – Tuer Cycles.

So whenever Punk missed a landing . . .

Then his 'friends' would move in . . .

They knew how to do that, all right.

They were quite happy to see him keep

bodging his jumps.

As we kept on practising the Dragon, the Chain Gang's jumps got better and better – and Punk's got worse and worse. Suddenly a group of cross-country riders came whooshing through . . .

. . . and there was a loud . . .

BANG!

One of the riders had a blowout. For some reason Punk and his crew thought this was very funny.

But their laughter stopped when the cross-country rider(1) whipped the old tube out,(2) zapped a new one in, then pulled a tiny compressed air cartridge out of his pocket and(3) stuck it in the valve and . . .

. . . instant inflation! Rider gone!

Awesome. Even Punk's dad seemed impressed. That night I saw the mechanics at Tuer Cycles working late.

Next day, everyone was back on the hill, training hard. Everyone except Larry, who was scrabbling around in the dirt.

Hey, everybody, look at this!

He was looking at a nutshell with a hole in it. Fascinating!

This hazelnut has been eaten by a dormouse. A very rare animal. You can tell because the hole it made has smooth edges.

We all crowded round to get a better look.

I thought it was pretty boring so I picked up Larry's binoculars.

Looking through binoculars the wrong way is cool. Everything looks like it's very far away. You feel really alone. Even all the other downhillers seemed to have gone. All except Punk coming towards me, but he was miles away. Or so I thought. Suddenly . . .

PPHHHWAPP!

It was the biggest jump we had ever seen!

So what did you think of that? Tyre-inflation cylinders connected to the pressure valves f front and back air-damped shocks controlled by a switch on the handlebars.

The following Saturday was the start of the two-day race weekend. We knew Punk would be using his compressed-air jumping system, so after our first runs we met up at the Dragon to check out Punk's run.

NNOOOOO

The front cylinder activated – the rear
one didn't. Result – a loopdeloop,
another smashed bike
and an angry
Punk.

On our way to lunch, we couldn't help overhearing the conversation between Punk and his dad in their race-support vehicle.

Dozy had to leave after lunch to help out at the family grocery store in town. Later, he told me what happened that afternoon.

23

Uncle Deepak got out his crystal ball.

Hmmm. I see somebody who thinks he can buy success and buy friends. I see someone who doesn't know the meaning of the word "teamwork".

Then he showed Punk one of his most popular tattoos.

This is the teamwork tattoo.

It shows a dragon crushing a warrior. He relied too much on heavy armour and weaponry. Nimble, lightweight warriors pin it down by working as a team.

Next, Uncle Deepak did a ball-point tattoo on Punk's arm to remind him to find some real friends.

That evening, Larry, Andy and I were getting in some last-minute training before the next day's race. We had done O.K. in the first race but not made it to the podium. Anyway, who should appear but . . .

Suddenly he seemed to want to be friends.

But Andy wasn't happy about my bad behaviour.

Andy was right –
if I beat a rubbish
opponent, then I would be
an only-slightly-less-than-rubbish winner.
First among losers.
I called Punk back.

OK, you win. I'll help you with your jumping. Do that small one over there for me first.

I saw his problem straight away!

CRUNCH!

OUCH!

He was roaring off
the lip, like a bag of
cement on wheels,
instead of pre-jumping it.

O.K., Punk, here's what you've got to do. ① Five metres from the edge, push down hard on the pedals and handlebars, compressing the springs. ② Then as you near the lip, let the springs rebound while you pull up. That's a pre-jump. It'll give you loads of extra height.

Punk learned fast. Soon he'd conquered
the Dragon.

BOINGG!

Sunday morning, race two, first run.
Punk would be the last one down so
after our runs we all met up again
at the Dragon to watch.
Uncle Deepak and his
mates were already
there.

Even the Chain Gang
cheered him.

The landing was perfect but . . .